Southwest Reconstruction

Southwest Reconstruction

Raquel Gutiérrez

NOEMI PRESS

Published by Noemi Press, Inc. A Nonprofit Literary Organization. www.noemipress.org

Cover & Book Design by co • im • press

ISBN: 978-1-955992-69-5

For Gata y Gorgeous

CONTENTS

if memory is the act of bearing witness . . . then the dream is a friend driving us somewhere

—Akilah Oliver

And then, on fire, as if the whole Pacific were burning, the breakers flashed and the glow of the waves over the horizon dyed the sky with the ancient red color of our flesh. When the waves soaked us and the skies made us seasick carrying us upward. When sobbing among the flames of the waters we felt ourselves move once again and it was all the seas, all the lakes and rivers, all the deserts and mountains burning into the sky as if the whole ocean were on fire as it became with us alive again and these waves were setting on fire our flesh with love.

—Raúl Zurita

AN INCANDESCENT UNDONE

There is a two-laned monstrous coming
What have I done?
    The juncture, a bearing.

The emission into the earth,
    the redder fruit, altars to the dead
    circle the cacti.

    It's a crossroads
    in my skin.

I have a distant cosmology, an oil to anoint against the sign of the cross.

There is a kinship unbecoming to me.

Departures

KING OF THE ROAD

Caminante,
to love is a dilation
        in need of wide open expanse

A wake of buzzards whisper
this road is the only home you know

To be unwanted is an origin story

There was nothing to fasten you in place
And with this much ache
You could bask in debt,
call it peace, or catch it

Staring in a rearview, igniting crux:
        to be seen or merely remembered

If you could only see
what they see as they set you off into
The same implacable horizon, a cloud ballroom
emerging in each mile marking regret

Irrepressible as color changing with the light,
the only reliable currency and
The only high that kept you rolling;
desperate for higher ground

In this mirage, this desert forded love
But the desert was love and you would soon
be the tornado that memory chased,

homes strewn with the ends of the future
                                        scorched in your wake

Where you unearth the assumption
about the way desires
were wrapped up in the leaving
                                        and so you always left
and that equation created
a canyon of want
and made the moving landscape your container

AND YOU WANTED TO SHOW ME THE MEXICO OF SLAUSON AVENUE

I missed you every day I lived there

I wanted to show you
exactly how
Food For Less
sits on top of
Sleepy Lagoon.
AztecaTV, Chicanx hotspot
pink wifi calibration,
a neon green brought
back and forth the border is painted a roof of paisa monstrosity

that's what makes loving me
the rawest material, wood made flesh
and the corrugated metal
that makes our ailing rain dulcet
no longer the barbarity
that comes with insolvency; a credit rating
ready to drop upon me, that when I wake
only to dream again that you were not fragile this time,
where Slauson Avenue is Mexico, an isle of noise worth waking for

THERE IS NO PLACE ELSE

I wanted North out of this highway

Pinching a roach out of this commute
between myself and the hungers shuttling
between gas prices and price surges;
I recall my room had a door

bolted from the outside
where the rents were high
and every end to the romance
left me on the brink of
                                        bankruptcies

I was an early investor in a dog
who refused to sleep in the bed with me
a rescue from the dreams made easy
to conscript into coordinates

I jump in my car again
I could look out and lament the hills and sky
usurped into screensaver
corrupted files and fantasies of indigeneity

I could not wait to be unsettled
by el camino real, its chatrooms
like its little bells on a pole were a show of might,
charming me into mestizaje;

4th grade curriculum
and the diorama my mother helped realize
when all I wanted was to bring

Mission San Juan Capistrano
back to the swallows

a messy song bird that could extract
the confession from my voice

SAN JUAN BAUTISTA

It had been a significant number of miles
by the time my parents broke down

My father never thought to tame his touch
in front of us, in front of me, a young sentinel
                                        at the foot of a faraway
Torn into film strip
where more imagined lives came too close
and the life I imagined kept hardening with each flinch

My mother guarding her breast
and exhaling all of the other choices beyond

This man who drank alone in the trailer
con coraje he staked his claim
by telling her she resembled Sophia Loren.

And she did
        as the sun poured
                into her side of the minivan

A bad omen like a dance craze.
A nice figure warding off curse
We sat in silence at the mouth of the mission,

My mother soured on the sweet fragrance
of the bougainvillea, a fetching shade
                                of purple on a trellis

It had always inspired her truest swooning

And none of this occurred to me as I was asked
to leave the van to see the mission by myself,
accompanied only by the disposable camera I carried,
practicing for the real thing one day.

I pointed and shot and knew
the image would mean something different
when I got older.

THE UNIVERSITY OF EL CAMINO REAL

Built by our forebears and their forbears
to be worn like skin

The legend metabolized into a theory
of the drum.

Collapse into the invitation
from a long lost relative forged in the fires

of the imaginary there was one,
A flor y canto etched into skin

Make a discipline out of its rhythms
or a retirement account that soars when
the country of our birth goes to war

Some relatives stay lost by design,
others get found in a literary movement.

The archive paid off my truck note.
What if it was all supposed
to remain on the page?

Instead of hinging a self to a history
of othering

a midlife teleology that would forgive me
when student loans refused to

It was another start of a schoolyear
where bombs dropped elsewhere

and the data machine
singes huipil with an ember of discrepancy

STAR IN THE LOS ANGELES RIVER TUNNELS

(after Star Montana)

A star above   our heads;

we look up and cross ourselves
under the sign of a black dress in mourning

we are born under the sign of contaminants
where the brunt of us is survival.

To look forward in the left behind, to cast
a gaze in the far afield where

A sad girl symmetry catches
the light and the light is stilled.

The river nips at your feet;
strong armed for tender embrace.

There is a soul framed
in the outline of the tunnel

Standing with an invisible stigmata

The tunnel and her tendrils,
There is an ache that rises like a flood

There are always shadows to allay
Las sequias del corazón

It is desire that drowns us

We become bridge for a train
that comes to see us on occasion.

Sometimes we are stuck   at the crossing,
and wait for it (all of it) to pass

RUINS, CHAVEZ RAVINE

(after Sandra de la Loza)

Who stood before the ayuntamiento?

Julián Chávez and all of his accent marks
over the graves of the dispossessed

A New Mexican patience for permission
to take the unoccupied tracts of land
to feast on the forgotten; a settler screams first
and is the last to be seen
as a founding father; marrying off
an ancient Yaanga (a place)

Yaangavit (a people) had a colonial encounter,
a trope needs rest
and housing in these hills have always known crisis

A friend in the present films the videos of the past,
moving images of young women being evicted
from their homes on his and her and their smart phone
to upload to their instant camera telegrams.

A commentary on the intermittent horizontal lines,
the graphical interference.

Who wonders about the evidence
of this displacement being sufficient.
Does anyone believe in the fact of seizure?

From this perch you can't see who is who
and who is fleeing or who is fighting
who is dreaming and who is plotting

and who is having a sobering conversation
about the future of their neighborhood

Who is studying tenant law, the bar exam;
an art of war when the lights go out.

The earth is still warm to the touch,
the day's heat steeped into the hillside.
El calorcito, even when the hill stops
living side by side its old neighbors.

The sun shines regardless of tenancy,
in spite of possession being nine-tenths of the law

There were those that dreamt inside humble homes
La Loma, Palo Verde and Bishop
Dreams that somehow eluded the grabbing hands
that latched to limbs,
wrists, ankles
twisting in the wind

and bound to the backseat of a police car,
watching their homes go up in value
when it was better to see them go up in flames

A SPECIES OF PRECARIOUS HOPPING

I fell for another coyote magic trick
now I am panicking like dogma
and chasing starcrossed patterns
hatched across an unaffordable sky
I was desperate for a place, any place
a yellow-red-white-and-black place
as every four directions boasts a nomad
and a hot tub under the stars
these are the mythological stripes
to a place to imagine, to play, and see to the future
coming in from the end of time to answer like a planchette
moving across the parade of a libertarian hinterland
This is what Joshua Tree gave me when my excess found austerity
when my heartbeat found consequence   in the body of Purifoy's assemblage
Here the moonsong dreamstutter   washing over Jumbo Rocks
until it disappears fuck me as a sun rocket cheers
inside another burning   pale blue pyre.
Here come the ancient good times   where I get pulled over
but a passport and a sage bundle bless me into the crossroad
I brought some toys for Eleggua   I love the unpaved roads of a high desert
with low interest rates the cool poverty, the acceptable shakes
like sex with private property
in the aging hipster economy   a five star review insures me to parties
like Manifest Destiny's Child

I might call on ritual to cut my way
out of this pack
when they try to turn my dog against me.

The familiar betrayal necessitates survival,
the first of many frontiers.

EVIL TWIN

(After North Twelfth Heaven, by Amina Cruz)

A flag and the skies
The parts and its labor

Frayed and beaten   but you see the
Don't Tread On Me
A snake hissing on a moth-eaten t-shirt
waving on a rebar pole poking
out of a transmuted ocean floor.

Home and hearth
and freedom

The image of the mind is the first to go.

These are the heavens for all who discover them

The one who makes cowlick into labrynth?
The one who raises their hand to bless your head?

In every bible there's the 40th night: when the desert leaves us
disoriented and then it leaves us again—
desperate for direction, grasping, meaning

Left to monger,
cartographer and map.

En los terrenos diablos
we find shelter,
and relieve ourselves with reinvention
from the seizures that signed our names.

There is brown noise on the radio.

In the threshold of the translucent dream
that infuses onto the saguaro,
the familiar sentinel with which we overidentify
in our pursuit for holy land.

In heaven there is no thirst
or hunger or pleading with life, or normalcy—
or the threat of antiquity by the simple pleasantries
that elude a quotidian life.

In heaven the oxygen is not privatized
where the desert makes these inequities
a tactile exercise, here is the hell
and all must pass through it,

and if you can cajole the desert's daggers
knowing you will, someday, reach water again,
evil twinning alongside cowboys we suffer
bathing fools made bright
while the night falls deep in ceremony.

Heaven in the desert
finds its goddess like truth
Marking you like wind
under skin and slander
on your name.

PERFORMANCE THEORY

One day I am boxcutting
my way through the overwhelm
such a sudden need to end scene

And I marvel as the concrete touches caliche

It is the seed of my worry,
it is the seed of my peregrination

I want to lodge myself in sediment
in a getaway car called language
and lay it all to rest

No more calls out of the shadow or the screen on the wall;
no more was it plausible that one could be loved
or that one might be loved
trapped in a freezer in the dead of winter
or trapped inside a sedan in the month before monsoon

A dangerous situation
practiced as a durational performance
as a requirement to stay in one place
as a means for your interiors
to strut in the mouth of expulsion

A FUNNY FEELING

I lived above an excavation of coarse olfactory pleasures,   the slaughterhouse
in my toxic barrio, a place students write papers about
and in beats between the factory death permeating the evening chill

I recall my father's labor episode at the Farmer John's and imagine
it was there where he got good at spraying down our driveway,
so efficient with the stream

I consider our bond broken before my arrival

How do you make sense of the county hospital
and its hospitable commons, a refuge
without the burden of being seen

My parents worry in one tongue
Maybe the schools in my neighborhood
should have shown
the lines on the map   to meet the citation of suffering,
where my ancestors   once crossed themselves
in the name of Jesus.

Social studies failed to realize my father left a Mexico for
another Mexico that evaporated before his arrival.

Isn't that why we leave? To get there before it is gone.

Bastard chances   taken in the shadows of a sacrament
What chance do I have   to decipher the scratches in the soil
long eroded before my arrival,   back in a time when the season crested
back in a time   when you would leave the house   before sunrise

LOSERS ON BOTH SIDES OF THE FAMILY

(after Laura Aguilar's Nature Self-Portrait #10, 1996)

Holding frontier like court,
a pock-marked terrain
upon butch hinterland.

Here, another queer landscape
to leave sacrifice in the aftermath
of its founding,
becoming in its reflection
a junk yard junction—

Lap up the water beside her,
its taste soaked in a poisonous mineral sweet enough
to forget yourself in the breach—

and in the land made cheap with grab, frack, and sap.

I'm a polemic for her blooming.

She slumbers like pecho y ombligo,
slipping softness into knotty pine.

I siphoned the trembling galaxy
inside her belly
and into my cavernous marrow,
subdued by the sediment.

Surrender.

Ingress

US VERSUS US

I drive all night

I am a Texas Eagle
I am a Sunset Limited
I am

hurrying a longhorn
skull summons over threshold
A mid-life high speed chase
to lose again someday

to say ours, a re-encounter,
could endure a broken down
swamp cooler

Another Southern Pacific
dust storm
and then another one
at the end.

Here come the trains
and June
has us wearing
our skins again

Nina Simone on my phone
prying her out
of these full-throated
speakers

My white t-shirt gasps goddamn suavecito
Tom Waits on Vicente
then more Nina on vinyl
(even the record player sweats)

An upcoming neighborhood

Where I could see
railroad tracks adjacent
where the money goes
worth one man who steals
19 heads of cattle
the fact Camp Grant Massacres

us into the egress of history

It put us against us
us versus us
sus tierras verdaderas

The Airbnb omits
that Eskiminzin had a reputation
as the leader of a nation
before blood became rational

he smelt fear among whites
Our desire, an arsenal
that deals fear against whites

I almost bled through my seersucker
pants and boat shoes

hungry coyotes
approve our hunt

You can take me anywhere
I meant to say with
Apache tears for all,
a conjuring stone for the disempowered

And our bodies,
our poor bodies
in constant rehearsal

Consecrating the landscapes
of ourselves
in perpetual motion

SONOITA MASSACRE

I had no love but love
and no occupation but labor

Reventon Ranch   primero de mayo 1859   seven Mexican workers
are whipped by their overseer.

I'm not turned on by normal power   Catholic church and seven sacraments later
This is why I call you, lover.
Cinco de Mayo is our safe word. It rings true.

Mercer shaved off their hair in a particularly brutal manner.
The Anglos blazing infinite.
Dickies and Cortez.

What I drink doesn't heal the cut on my belly, what I snort cuts the cord between cortex
A warning warm moaning, a vision

As these settler bros approached a mescal distillery   how to preserve dignity
down on my knees
my country piss on me

We had no government, no taxes, no public debt.
Just nature

Mexican and Yaqui workers
an attemped escape   a broken sullen fire
too busy to be dreaming here, a place of commerce   an assemblage mob of seven armed
men
four Mexicans, one Yaqui lay dead

Sonora Mining and Exploring Company

just us miscarriage   in the building of state out of frontier
that followed Arizona's captain extractive industries captive with
years to come
years to yonder

but I'm lazy for money, imagination
A rage in my womb.

HELP ME LORD IT'S GETTING HARDER

We are the desperate Does
slipping back and forth
the border. We go astray to commit our crimes.

My co-signer sabotaged   231 males living in Tubac
23 males born outside Mexico, and now there is
a New Mexico territory with one drop of Spanish blood
for all of us to share in like ejído.

Posten bragged of paternalism,
claiming that he married Mexican couples
baptized their children   denied literacy marrow for

fluid work patterns of the caliche underground
another desert bucolic before getting into the union.

I turned 40 inside you and still living at home
the last bites of artisanal breakfast torta
were hard to swallow

after getting laid off I just wanted to go home

Texas cross index tonto didn't know
you weren't exactly from Mexico

a mean abuela who yells *You're not fucking me right!*
                    and the right belongs to all

where private property and market exchange rings,
where to go when there is nowhere to go, when to go politely after
the choke down robbed you of years.

I thought this was the place I could come home

Disculpa
I was mistaken

THE SIN OF BOREDOM

A daddy fetish placed upon 1910

when Father Hidalgo marches through the land

white ducktail and dick in his hand, fingers fast fretting.

I feel sad for his flag.

History makes poverty the example,

you are too much except when you are too poor. A gaslit sonata.

Reflex and spirit   hide the garbage behind a secret door—

We reside in the same room as rotting.

I drop sweat into the star crossed

class war, a recycling bin there, done that

It's before noon and taxes

when I watched you smoke   your cigarettes up my cunt

glowering morning strumming   the same two guitar chords all night long.

Blowing piñon through the keyhole.

smoke wings break into a bedroom borrowed a blanket disavowal warmth broken

so badly I renamed myself calamity.

THE CAT BATS FERAL AT THE CROSSROAD

I purr my cholo polo   Art Laboe chuliando
for seclusion, epigraphs and dedications
to *please come home* on the radio,

on my way to watch
you water plants in black straps
I unearth your new skirt, a built environment,
                                        concrete on nopal—

I fondle the market imperative.
We fuck on real estate manuals,
federal guidelines, enabling acts, and court rulings—

Survive 2008 today every single day with me,
my poverty, my penance, my fantasy escape hatch.

I could get by on the imaginary, and retire to what hasn't been spoken

There are no more cultures left to broker   sin luz en la calle

as we leave what desires us in the loam,
take in peace to fight each other
for each other's vaccine markings,

remove flags from each others' ass,
and tape fake cacti to each others' frente.

Or laugh and say we did.

WOULD IT KILL ME TO BE A NICER GUY?

We sign our lives away
in poems that announce the populations
of the middle of somewhere,
a high noon called midnight. Another howling
Coyote ass chorus of disapproval—Malinche
was my Farrah Fawcett poster
no strap no thong no tongue just hair
on my big bad brown teen lobo
bedroom wall for real.
The gigalo furrowed browed jowls
an estrangement with my pack
of sancho sinvergüenzas
who weren't interesting enough for Mommy Malinchismo
But we appreciate over time, these papers, an archive.
So for a good time call Cortez, a casual encounter.
No strings attached, cuando estoy triste I swipe right.

RESTRUCTURAL

A disintegration in your hands
spilled spheroid in an open capsule,
remaining still
alongside the petitions,
of El Tiradito's wishing wall.

I want to be seen in a sunset
of the thereafter, to recall
these unnameable years;

how we occupied the time
with new ways
to occupy the worry, a preoccupied
permission granted
as ours and ours alone.

Commiting to each other,
like one brick
on top of the other,
a slow building in the making.

GESTATIONAL EMISSIONS ON SUNSET BLVD

the creatures
we need for tonight's
atavistic sunset,

are stars in the bark
we eat and eat
to induce new cascades,

a yellow bile, your new skirt
a power pleat folds
like savior labia

you say you will save me
and then dump my body
in the river ángeles

the next incantation,
your book of spells,
where you tell

a hacendado
the truth and then
forget you did

WOUNDED DESERTER

I deserve your kyanite
finger flipping me off

Thorn the stud finder
all the way down

this frontier's skin
finding its ways

into my own skin
to conspire against

myself again. Here is
a refusal to register

touch with cognizant dog star
passed and dignified

my fugitivity, new planets
one winter broken in two

as neon spring awaits
a neo-con summer

I hide but there's no shade
but the shadow I fall in

EMOTIONAL LABOR

I wear you down like mammalian powder,
masticate you like time
fight the tempt   to reconcile
the cavern of your maw

Spread eagles
in the avarice. A crater,
to plumb and plunge.

We get blood on the sheets again.

I was the stone sundered into sex,
a quarry yawning inside   a mouth crusting with phosphate,
the earth evaporated for stray and starry scoria;

the pine cones pleaded
and their saplings never saw geminids
or perseids or the fiery tails
that promise me restless tresses laid bare
on the concrete parts of a national park.

I could barely move,   forget   the viscuosity
          of younger forests between thumb and forefinger,

You took the pulp for granted
and when I gave you a taste you bucked   medallion wild on bare breasts
                                                  backlit by sun as if for the first time ever
                                                                                  there was time

Spasm sought nipple
For I, mere boscage and eager chaparral,
        never learned to keep my wailing at bay.

You didn't give me back. You took an axe and thought about it
        and said I had jouissance but I didn't have a job.

I was kindling in your arms.

YOU PAUSED AND TURNED AROUND INSIDE

The adobe house that hid us
inside its address, 666 in the barrio,
the number of the beast,
it was an underworld we concocted
a safe word we agreed to, a safe word
we kept forgetting and laughed each time
we tried to recall the password that snapped us
out of this eager eros, of so many
scenes we have always dreamt of,

we took turns on our knees
staring at the selenite
on the windowsill.
I watch my tiny death flicker on loop

Where I come from no one bristles
at these obsolete belief systems
when a lover dares to call on you, siren
there are no boundaries to what binds us,
a history leathered in pain

You don't play Lotería with beans and shit,
you don't risk pleasure in the den of thieves but then again

There is nothing better than this recognition so
we smuggled ourselves into the goddamned

from this moment onward
there is no going back

THE BAR IN MY NEIGHBORHOOD

We walk into the bar and I am flooded
by the stink of disinfectant, the sight of deviled eggs

how to cast doubt on the edenic, a false god
the bible chaff, and many a vagrant attachment

I yawned the best years away waiting to find ourselves
as lovers in a land lording over us   scraping flesh from our rind

I remember losing sight of you as I made conversation
with a terrible man and his problems unaware by the fragility of it all

I am prideful in my fractions
a comeback kid

Deference to the jukebox, brown liquor anxieties
there is only so much a code of flesh can do to provide cover

This is the place that warns me of a future where
I am dead in my tracks or I could die on the tracks

The Buffet is one of the oldest bars built to serve
the workers of the nearby railroad depot in the Iron Horse district of Tucson.

In the morning on my way to work, I was always seized by the impulse
and picked up the rusty spikes lazing in the overgrown grass

of the neighborhood's sidewalks. Touching these objects touched
by these men, sitting on the barstools of an underworld. And me,

stuck with my tendency to wander

MY TEETH BREAK THE ICE

against anxious paywalls in disguise
A susurration of the wind
scratching out of its own skin,
a pillage. Conquer the remaining moisture
from my hands, my sex, my seven falls,
are fingers in the middle of surviving these fissures again.

We shift tectonic
The stone erodes the obedience;

Tonguing fire, molten Nicorette
birthing flowers in my pores
for memory to graze on the nervous system
we come back from the part of the dead we sprung from

here we come on winged eyelids and butterfly knives
Barbara Lynn East Texas southpaw
Fender maple playing angel has beckoned us, a pack between
three-quarters Mexican hot pink   just try it, Daddy

You want to bring out
the cholo in me

Call me chulo
one more time

Misremember this tenderness that chase
these blues away
affect and affix   your hand, poised

I was the velvet this time

AN UNCONSCIOUS REDIRECTION OF FEELING

You told me a child would be lucky.
Paperthin wetness, I pray along each bead of sweat
Madre nuestra glisten for this petition;
for each square of toilet paper sticks to my skin.

I meant this, baby. I want to baby you
You see this baby growing inside me? I do it for you.

Chained up stomping at the circus.
You held me from your side of the prison wall,
and I am another Dumbo inside the safe and warm
shelter of your trunk.

It doesn't look right but that's how it feels—
you locked away and me here—disgraced by my desire

The ringmaster forces his ring on you
The rose quartz comes cloudy when you come,
bellowing sudor y nadie te manda.
If mother father universe could see me fly,

over piñon and ponderosa the younger.
And you.
Another distance not to come, obscuring fruit.
Bosc the browner, their sweeter seeds

We can fly fast reaping a togetherness grown inside me,
sometimes I come by it honestly despite
a vacant womb.

Let me swoop rescue under the weight of this scrutiny.

THERE IS A MOTH IN MY LAZY POMPADOUR

Passing through Gates Pass
The barrios get smaller
with consumptive views
Imbued with not even
You can take this
Panoramic away from me.

Even when you're not here—you are mine.

A diuretic prophecy, a golden
beauty shuffling my syntax.

This was a temporary sun,
A signal assuring me
it was never the lesser
but it was once real.

Desire is the axiom
It shows up unannounced and
its potential for secret latrines
and dirty convivial greetings
with grin and groin
get me into trouble.

Such gusto.
Con mucho.

Did you know
That the universe
Is always already
A voyeur?

Your darkness swarmed
And I consented
But the moth in my mouth
Showed me
How to gargle light.

UNTITLED: SUB-TITLE

(after Laura Aguilar's "Nature Self-Portrait #4, 1996)

Sleep combustible
a fiery belly flop head first
in the rising disks that pass for clouds around us.

A breached birth,
submission in surround sound
she must have loved me,
with the cord around my neck.

Here a gesticulation dosed with kaleidoscope filament,
charms my phantom tail
It is the part tamed with touch,

and tone-policed when I yelled
her name en la calle, a common cualquiera.

Come inside the house now she said.
Donde saco su cuchillo, pointed to my belly
and murmurred *mío*

She scratched my back, pouted bitemark into shoulder blade,
lullled me into the undulating concave of her restless bombtick.

She said I brought her calm. I saw her suck her thumb.

I LAID MY EYES UPON HER

I was the stone that unsettles birthing canals my lavaswells
I am liquid metal   unbecoming.

She stubborns the quarry that used to let me cut her hair— I, the little purple flower on her finger.

A gorgeous engorged atoning.
A gorgon once named
far-roaming, a road widened,
concrete, forceful and ruler. Was she even mortal?

I was six seeds of pomegranate
that grew seasons in her belly
she wintered away from me interned
in a coma of her making

How does she do so much each day, every day she is beheaded.

It's hard to compete with the West
so we settle the crux and a coin-operated conversion.

She does laundry every day and threatens to leave when Cruzando complains.

She hands serpent her reign. Milk skin lengua when my back is turned.
Taking handfuls of arid madrecita.
She wouldn't recognize me without a deed,
fingers too fallow for the abandoned sand.
Soft matter too soft to turn stone, stone turned over to profit.

Sometimes I look back at her land—was she a temple or a grave?

SUPPLICATION

I had given over to charlatan

Sully the water with lust again,
a dying Springsteen at the end of his immolation

Upon a hologram in heat, I recollect:

holding your dress open,
a butch grammar taking over.

Rubescent an oil to plunder,
a terrain lays in wait

I never take the time to tend to those
open and deep.

PERSON ANOTHER

person who is not
my person anymore.

Who keeps you anchored in the neoliberal thinness,
an abscess in the year of cautery where
my skin breaks unique

these ways lubricate
a here among the creosote   can you feel its balm
I rub on the parts that burn like

rubies we didn't   suspect in the wash   another full moon rose above the crux
where I buried your ring
outside casita pedaling city limits you will find me in
the one place you could   never bring yourself
          to call home.

Mine is a ritual's scepter
I use to pat down the soil
firmly into the fissure
three times to make sure

the skin I sleep in is mine.

CALL OFF THE DOGS

in the garden and refrain from weeding the flowers
you call weeds,

break the tar down in my lungs
sweet mugwort mugwort bitter

salve in the mugshot
of my alkaline.

The Spanish arrive like clockwork
turn the page history book where it all looks the same

it's late 17th century, the Tohono O'odham permanent villages these waterways

were systems   a flourishing. We let go of Tucson last,
Mexican troops on the ground
two thousand farmers   1856 (almost ten

years after Guadalupe Hidalgo),
I know you say annoyed as fuck

you know everything that
spills off the parchment
about what used to be Mexico.

Gadsen Purchase
for the New York relatives,
El Tratado de la Mesilla
for the Royal Aztecs, vatas locas purple nylon sheen,

Despegate de tu vaga settler wanderings come home already
only you can save me
when you touch me with the tips of your fists.

ORE FORGIVENESS

Mica eye, rose quartz
carnelian
moonbound and moribund
but tonight
I gotta let it go

There is no new nmemonic,
nary a crag to test my recall,
dig a hole and fake my death
when I wasn't sure
the deviled winds would come to pass.

I roll tobacco to fill the time
to fill the vessels with my pang cloud,
pluming toxic feathers tickle
the parts of me that need translation

let me not explain these antibodies
sisterlife brotherdream smuggle me
in heirloom curves filled with eros,
depression pink glass perfume bottles

a sorrowing carmine
that makes my water blush

rushing walls inside a brooch
the sweetest sweat dew windows
the sauna hourglass that burns alive
as my wind stone clears my path

EL GORDO Y EL FLACO

Hello my absent other,
come loosen my authority
and corroborate the situation
you haphazardly created for yourself.

You saw the blue car in the South side of town today,
it was near the park, there was no driveway.

These are the tiny indignities
that tighten your grip around el gordo
and then el flaco, The Dicks in your repertoire,
a prized possession, play “Lifetime Problems”
on loop.

A queer punk rocks my phantom limbs who
ask about you in those forlorn hours
when you take them out of their coffins,

they wonder if your handshake loosens
before or after you come home
as you play the failed scene over again
while the key turns the lock, and the door
jams and creaks and the light flicks on

You groan silently
at being seen

HORIZON AS SEEN FROM A PLANE, A CHEAP FLIGHT

a window seat | an aisle to the potentiality | an underbite | another day we line with loss | you remember José and so do I | several posts in one day | signal a manic episode | it doesn't equate the stillness you boasted about | through the burning line cutting across these unprepared worlds | you woke me from dream | to tell me plaintively that you were thinking about loss again | you are writing an essay | "to think through" | how you missed me so much | like my dream wasn't the only place I encountered you | it is the only place I encounter you | so I rush off to sleep | and now when I look out the window for once not my phone | the red lightens into a soft fiery coral | softening to the thick white thread | between today and a blurry evening shy like it still doesn't know | how to come in from out the cold | with shoes off now | walking barefoot | as if not to scare you off to that place you go | where the sun blocks me | but I follow the aura of your crown | and no one will be able to say it to you the way I say it to you | and you will always seek me out across time zones | like you do when no one is looking | that is where you want to live | with me | in the vanishing point | and no guessing | let me tell you everything

Ascension

CORONA

And then there is the drive back to Tucson
just before Picacho heralds
the last remaining 40 miles to my bedroom;

It is a place where my sins get named and packed
up in the attic of my mind wandering the highway
as my foot on the gas pedal allows it to consider
the moot nature of a rosary bead unless its pressed roses
and then it feels like all is forgiven and in syncopated
time I welcome the night in the sideview mirror
to spirit me away while my body earns its keep
as co-pilot. I make the choices and my passenger
absorbs the shock of consequence like a good wingman,
for a road trip is a dress rehearsal for the real thing.

THIRST TRAP IN THE GLOAMING

Commuting towards mountains in silhouette
        pat down a discount barber school cut along a pink neon line
    tracing its finger down muscle, taut terrain in formation,
        a bothersome cavalcade of ranges named after saints.

how lonely I was and nothing masculinity could do about it
hiding on Election Night, the darker it gets outside
    and the interior closing in on me.

I document every movement like stations of a cross
        for the full moon promise of staying young, getting laid

            a reluctant human sacrifice, bongwatered into fruition
                by the time another cycle completes.

The night is purpling into lumpy tissue, a breast to dissect. My god
    the good choices
        are getting harder to decipher

There will be eczema intuiting over and over, scratching into soil,
a hot screed truth serum

but in the meantime to ward off the bad winds and
all that took to come here, without you—

I write my book, angel

ON WINGS

our feet
or bellies east
to where we follow
the fickle sun
bison be afraid

we are stealing pills that got us touching
hiding amphetamine under tongues

the cold calm refines when it comes
and the medicine cabinet opens on the landing
corroborating my rival's prediction that Columbia
would graze the prairies unencumbered.

I found you in the middle of the night. Remember?

White toast and butter settles our grief
and ignores our hungrier days.
Lace dances on our backs
where we were conquered

A best western karaoke lounge,
ideals and up on knees
for the Zapata mustache tickle where 1910 lies sullied
by the reminder that Texas arranged hangings like mealtime

HOW MEXICAN IS MEXICAN?

(after Laura Aguilar)

An identity and a family
is a social sculpture for critique,

a kinetic motion for a composite, of the bloodline;
and all the little ways we mistake each other for kin.

Four directions for remaining on good terms
with one's own skin

What are the terms of engagement,
the maternal spikes at the nerve's ending

Sunken eyes sink a ship off the shore of the San Gabriel watershed;
I am ready   for possibility?

Minus the monument erected to the *what will they say*
When I attend to a Mexico seen in the dreams of these walls

A portrait in three, four of me. 1, 2, 3, and the one you don't see.

A ring is a promise, a cue and a curtsy in this familiar sight of play.

All of these years against all of these eyes
and I still resisted asking for permission

to dream in ancient symbols

A language jostled in my sleep as
my ancestors resent the inquiries

the way that I endure the double takes in my direction
like a theater of mestizaje and the montage

where the protagonist overcomes the perils, the last act concludes
with authenticity gnashing its teeth

I.
There,
a new path
to tread

with each step
a new signature
through your
concrete structures.

Clouds mantra,
in billowing perpetuity.
Singular Texas sky,
dust damned to bedevil.
A solitary occasion
like a mile
in my shoes, a stretch.
And me, a sullied t-shirt.

The art of brown labor.
Donald Judd.
Vista convergence,
a study in ego.
Grief for the concrete.
rafa esparza.Self-love
in lowercase, a practicum.

The loss is language
of the landscape
A bridge in the gap.
Mando's Burger.
Too much mustard,
red gold.

I am mourning what
I began to articulate—
a queer brown
future. I let go,
heave hostility
in its stead.

I arrived with
attending fanfare;
the institutionality
of the resistance
to the art market
is romantic.

Pioneers remade
the local military
architectural history
into a means to
vacate destination.
The body
of the artist
dies and the labor
dies too though
not immediately
but the artwork
gets to live
forever.

I came to forget you
only to see you
on the other side
of right angles,
coming together,
to make a world.

Tried for oblivion
under the Marfa lights.

I walked through
the concrete structures.
They didn't look like
they came from the land.

Do I look that way?

The landscape
was animated
by kinship. Still.
Split open
by the imposition,
a border. A border
was placed upon
land and dermis,
a scene of kin
comes dictated.
Rules served one
with landlessness
and unfair labor.
Is it hard to remember
or easy to forget
the thing you love.
A museum reminds
us daily. These are
thinking bodies
coerced again.
With *buddy,*
ma'am, watch your
head, not your
lucky day.

Where does this
concrete come from?
Poured into forever
molds, right angles
beget more right angles.   Far right.

Are we far enough?
90 degrees meeting
each other in multiples
of four. Quadrant
replication. You seem
functional but I question
your utilitarianist
ability.

Can you help me?

II.
I thought of you
as soon as my car wheels
made it an hour
West of El Paso.

I held off as long as I could.

I was in a Texas
finally legible to you.
I saw the Milky Way
touching its way
through the infinite bruise.

I rolled my car window
down and shouted your name
into the whirring engine;
a gradient of midnight blues.

When will we run out of color
shining with pearly stars?

I said your name.
I said your name again.
I said your name.
I said your name again.
I took a step.

A weedy patch,
a landing strip
in the middle
of the pathogens
between each
concrete structure.
Those structures
felt defiant at first
as though they didn't
care about whether
or not they belonged
on the land.

SAN ANGELO CITY LIMITS

I drove the misery only a panhandle
is capable of, a West Texan mystery
towards a portrait of a self in front
of the San Angelo City Limits sign

a sky at my feet a flatness
matched by the way I use "moon"
to describe my face before she forgets it,

Cursing a dirt road for 60 miles
to find my way back to my beloved

La hija de Genaro emerged from the Concho Valley,
in a super 8 film wearing white, a hellion

queen of her cousins, empty Coke bottles her crown.
Grandpa Chico sneaks them to her under the table
—everyone can see. His affection a rough rasp that billows
in the nape of her vellicate, her baby Texan drawl rains
like a fictionalized accountworth dying for.

Little girl shrieks toothsome,
makes a mockery of Chico's sediment tongue,
an accent that prefaces bells and sales of petrol,
the best in San Angelo   where all of their kin
can trace their line, a sturdy parallel warding off junction

I'm looking for Chico's gas station, like a tourist looking
for the only ghost in this town
full of chains and boxes

Her hair falls down long and straight
like the narrative of quantum the state dictates
and the scar along the trail beneath a mutinous chin,
an errant wandering.

The little girl in the film makes no sound,
I realize during another sunless morning.

A ROAD OPENER TO ROOT MYSELF RED

Be more reverent   we are all babes to break open and walk a red road.
Be less and heed the infernal woman, she who consecrates your dime,

Weaves webs and tsk-tsk separation spells towards a new plot, a softer hell,
a discounted metaphysics, or the Guadalupana altar inside the Food City.

A red clay below her hardened feet comes sticky like today,
a humid glue I pull out of the sky's cunt, her grito misconstrued.

This is where the the Gem Expo brings us what's been kept
deep inside mines and mines and yours, pussies unearthed besides

a high priestess card reversed. I wake inside the folds
of skin touching membrane that coat my tongue, unravel keloid

undo the braided embrace. Our mothers called
them scars, a star map of our bodies. I have an app to see them

when I hold up my phone to my heart. I have no other means to fake
the taking of flight into the ohm vortex, the dirt below the little cities above

where I needed you. They said it was taking me alive, this peppered want.
And to conquer it I must bury it and leave it unmarked.

ON THE DESERT FLOOR, AN OCEAN

It was my first fibroid occasion
where champagne pushes and percocet
cons my chakras into misbehaving again.
Racking up debt cysts on my fainting
couch knowing full well I have people
coming over with soup and the feeling
I had in the washed out moonlight spilling
into my living room was not verifiable.
Don't be afraid. The loneliness suits me,
the little trickster. I am doing my best to resist
the temptation of cynicism;
Movement in time breaks hours
and change like breakers flay the tide.
In a dream there is no kiss me on the lip
of a broken earth blistered by desire
The jealous pit holds secondhand echoes
of song, a dark howl vigil
Nobody cares pero no hay pedo.
I audition the brink, seethe in new flavors,
ride the edge again and steady
myself on serrated washes and watch the waves
brave these estuaries, I watch how floods flash
and flee, how oceans evaporate
and soar to the sky islands north of you.
On the day you came back I was still
empty handed when my chakras conned me
into balancing the distance that navigates the mundane;
just as the monsoon breaks the heat of waiting,
the fever of my toxic patience.

FLUENT DRAGON LUSTER, A DESERT DIVINATION

I hit the brakes on a broken wingspan   that stretched along Interstate-10
los angeles y tucson, los angeles to tucson
I resent this birth in the rearview;

leaving behind my big city nationalism
and bystander cheerleading   for the less deserving siblings

It feels terrible to let myself have what I want

I drive and read these roads
The desert could be my temple in the way
that the desert is just a mine

I'm here to claim the dead my psychic swears belong to me—milemarkers
focused on the distant ancestor washed ashore from her tribe;
I codify accordingly and wait for the a tribe to find me, claim me,
                                        love me, and protect me.

This is a common desperation
marking terrain like another car rolling,
reporting a speed trap. Declaring citizenship to the young woman in uniform.

A map is unfolding upon sordid heavens, Thomas Guide thunder soaked,
birthwet parchment sticking to my windshield

The ancestor in the bedrock of the unseen move through the ethers
While I pray to the headlights against the backdrop of a dark night.
Another dark night. Every night gets darker
                              and harder to see out of alone

CONTIGUOUS NOWHERE

Coyote pelt makes hiding
        in the morning brush difficult
it's laid out brutal bare; no artifice minus
        the mural of a two lane highway

A common king parses the atomies
        from a Sinaloan nightshade;

I sigh your name
in the prickly cholla
an ambush I come by honestly

I'm me again.

Two snakes in the incandescent address
of what is present, to chase into hollow burrow
the loose litter where all creatures are seen.
Come be seen with me predator,
naked we can roam visible and hardy,
the hardest won beauty He always does.

Aerate the Sonora fauna of tender you tell me.
Rebirthing tones to greener, more fragrant
less colonized no alibisjust be verdant and slow, leafy and open—no.

Hurry up and bloom,
attack the sunnier personas
that snarl our water.

DILUTE DEMOCRACY

Not to flail on the nomenclature
of an isolationist impulse
but the whites of this interior
suffer the tyranny of a democracy

And my fantasies are disintegrating alongside
the next government shutdown. No rest area is safe,
no library enshrined
and since we are the best
                    brown babes they ever did see
                    they keep their mitts on us
                    and now we have our memories
                                        erased and have to fight
                                        our own water ways   back to each other.

It is their party after all and our eavesdrop
is our pot luck and everyone wants to extract
monument valley where lightening
charges this sedimentary formation with pink electrons

and no one bothers to fact check their belly full
of lies or double agency
to re-settle our indian problems before the award is rescinded
and the ayayotes returned to their rightful heir

What happened to the fantasies of collective alliance?
Toasting to the enemies of the state.

These are the jobs I want to take away
clog the tributaries,
                    sully their veins, traffic the main artery

Dilute and dilute again
until the democracy
in our blood
cries uncle

CHICANOS PRACTICE MAKES PREROGATIVE

Cronos is the one.
eats half-white children, whole

green feather, blood fang
survive, alright?

ombligo stitched together,
on my leather belt

Cronos is the same
mates with brown women

in a desert that seeks capital,
where suns rotate closer

and codex eviction, daughter
of a television snowstorm

side-saddle and bareback
leathered once again.

father unhinges braces
from her chubby legs

buys time to defy, and swallow
sibling clay come to life

it's me. I embrace white divine
full body flavor living in an urn

a matrilineal burn, a beast we pick up
and leave again

PURO DESEO

There goes a mountain   afraid to lose its place   in the landscape.
A spinning   top the many lands   a patient inventory.
Inhale comfort from these contested terrains,   extracting answer
for a question coming into focus.   A dream of the theorist showed up
wearing a wine-hued plaid sky, a blue wind-breaker
smiling like a bulldog,   silver-lined and lionized, who sighs watching
the light fall over a tenuous hold of an Aztlán   so powerful
the people thought the page was king.

Is this how you imagine his face   when he looks to Picacho Peak and says
You should always be with the people you love the most.

I stumble through
the memory of the lover
who kept me off the streets,   away from el camino real,
I was suddenly a needle plucked from cholla
as an ocotillo passes judgment in this tiny
desert town.   These are the wild trails
where I temper a performative nature,
I move like a 45 record to groove,   and slither the erasures
In these discursive fantasies the pages are dog-eared,
well worn and masculine.
It was the year we saw the inexpressible   hovering in the distance.
We sat on our perches
to catch sight of children in cages
It could be the year we gave the lands back   and cleave our losses
with murmurs stuck in the back of our throats.

CARRYING OUT THE FIRST STEPS IN REPAIR

And when does it become unfathomable
this idea that we continue to soak
in the bedtime story of indigeneity,
to study the self in the skirt of serpents,
to follow the law of softness enabled
by the spoils of the state and her institutions,
What the removal led to—a dowsing rod assembly line
to divine the last traces of an ancestor who chooses
to remain lost and unfocused.

Something shifted in me
when I began to declare
the mestizo settler sat inside me

It broke me open to admit
it was the mestizo settler driving
this hand-me-down into the valley below

This whole time,
the mestizo settler
said hello to the destination
in the absence of armor—
where bone, muscle and stone intertwine.

A butterfly alights on my crow's feet
and I get to let go of an intoxicating
sense of belonging to the underpinned
and to fashion myself a lightshow instead

How distant this everyday passing for real   this life where epistolary novels
and cocktail glasses are imprinted   with red-red healing

I promise to dispel the myth to myself, to stop before I wager
the four directions and all of the names I have massacred on my tongue,
                                                                  even from a respectful distance

Skewing the data otherwise.

I FIND YOU IN THE JUNCTION, BABY

I plan a road trip every day before I go to work before
I fall off en route and the Santa Fe line on time
before you came along and I was not the fool fancied
suited and booted on a turn,

I fall off en route and the Santa Fe line on time
where I wander into the itinerant textual head space,
gall stoned in a museum of bordello arts,

I wander into the itinerant textual head space,
and think about the selfie that could save the world
a hole in my atlas, my hand rattling free that at last

I could be free of the selfie that could save the world
or practice deletion and thought again and then concrete,
recalled the fear of height in a multi-tiered parking structure

I thought against the concrete, recalled
a cliff's edge too well through a hole in my rearview,
so many cars like a freeway in heaven

too well to recall through a hole in my rearview,
it is all I ever wanted to show me the way back home
like Almaraz exploding cars, kerosene dreamfire spilling.

All I ever wanted was for you to show me the way back home
or do you need the poet's biography to glean a cry for help?
it's been walled out of me this ability to insist to strangers how

A biography is a map of tears.

NOTES ON THE TEXT

KING OF THE ROAD was inspired by the scene of Jack Twist crying in his truck while driving through the Wyoming landscape, only to arrive and be rejected by Ennis Del Mar, in Ang Lee's *Brokeback Mountain (2005).*

AND YOU WANTED TO SHOW ME THE MEXICO OF SLAUSON AVENUE takes a cue from Caliban who describes his locale as being "full of noises, sounds, and sweet airs, that give delight and hurt not," in William Shakespeare's *The Tempest.*

STAR IN THE LOS ANGELES RIVER TUNNELS is an ekphrastic work in response to the photography of Los Angeles-based artist, Star Montana.

RUINS, CHAVEZ RAVINE is inspired and in response to the documentary photography of Los Angeles based artist, Sandra De La Loza, whose work relates to the Chicana/e/o/x histories and communities that inhabited these important Chavez Ravine neighborhoods, early 20th century stewards of unceded Tongva lands. I write about the early Hispano settler, Julián Chávez, who in the 1830s petitioned an early council known as the ayuntamiento, to take control of unoccupied lands in what was Chavez Ravine and its most known inhabitant today, Dodger Stadium.

A SPECIES OF PRECARIOUS HOPPING makes a loving gesture to the assemblages by Noah Purifoy, located at the Noah Purifoy Desert Art Outdoor Museum, in Joshua Tree, California.

US VERSUS US references the 1871 massacre of 144 Pinal and Aravaipa Apache people by a group composed of United States Americans, Mexican, and T'Oho-no O'odham vigilantes. This was two months after the Apache, under the leadership of Chief Eskiminzin, surrendered to Lieutenant Royal Whitman who commanded Camp Grant for the U.S Army. Eskiminzin later shot and killed his friend in a show of strength to his tribe that no white man should or could ever be trusted.

SONOITA MASSACRE opens with lines culled from the diary of George Poston, known as the father of Arizona and founder *of the* Sonora Mining and Exploring Company. This poem references two incidents in 1859 in Tubac, AZ, where a white labor manager named George Mercer whipped and cut the hair of seven Mexican workers for an unknown transgression. Mercer shaved so closely that skin from the mens' scalps were cut, provoking outcry from the community. Days later two Mexican ranch hands stole livestock after killing their white supervisor with an ax, prompting a team of seven white vigilantes to search for those responsible for the murder. The vigilantes sought revenge and indiscriminantly killed four Mexican workers and one Yaqui at the distillery at Mescal Ranch. Details of these events can be be found in an article titled "Filibuster on the Sonoita," published in the online archive, *Baja Arizona History*.

HOW MEXICAN IS MEXICAN? is an ekphrastic work in response to the photography of the late Los Angeles-based artist, Laura Aguilar.

I FIND YOU IN THE JUNCTION, BABY makes reference to the artwork of the late, Los Angeles-based visual artist, Carlos Almaraz.

ACKNOWLEDGMENTS

Since 2015 these poems have haunted the attics and basements of my psychic space where desire and memory meet. It wasn't until I arrived in Tucson, a year later, that I could give flesh to these lines, many of which were workshopped under the care of my first poetry teacher, Joshua Marie Wilkinson. I was very happy when the University of Arizona Creative Writing MFA Program accepted me, and helped corroborate my inkling that poetry could be a life to inhabit full-time. An enormous well of gratitude for my brilliant cohort of poets—Gabriel Dozal, Gabriel Palacios, and Kou Sugita—my brothers in lyrical experimentation and intimate readers of my early drafts. Our cohort benefited from the ideal creatively healthy environment that the second year poets Claire Hong, Claire McLane, and Peyton Prater Stark had forged and stewarded before our arrival. I am forever grateful for that labor and your comradeship that enabled such a rich space for play, practice, and self-interrogation. I also wish to honor Susan Briante, Brandon Shimoda, Farid Matuk, Ander Monson, and Manuel Muñoz, as they were extraordinary guides and mentors during this journey of poetry making.

Anthony Cody was my editor and I was fortunate to find in him a fantastic and rigorous reader who encouraged me to imagine greater heights to soar and deeper inquiries to make over the course of these last two years. Carmen Giménez was the acquiring editor for this collection and I am grateful to her for adding me to the Noemi Press family. Thank you to Mariah Bloch and Sarah Gzemski for ensuring with aplomb that all the parts keep moving at Noemi Press.

Several of hese poems appeared in early and final forms in the following publications: *A Dozen Nothing*, *The Tiny*, *Quarterly West*, *Foglifter*, *Contraviento*, *Zócalo Public Square*, *Hayden Ferry Review*, *poets.org*, and *MĀNOA: A Pacific Journal of International Writing*. I wish to thank editors from these literary journals, magazines and web platforms for their attention to my work: Pete Mitchell & Jeff Sirkin, Gina Myers, Matty Layne Glasgow, Luiza Flynn-Goodlett, Claire Hong, Collette LaBouff, Joel Salcido, Brian Blanchfield, and Anthony Cody.

This manuscript was the document I worked on and revised during a deeply generative residency with Headlands Center for the Arts. I am grateful to the stewards of that institution and appreciate the daily care given to me by Holly Blake, Tesar Freeman, Damon Little, Ryan Seiter, Stephen Steinbrink, and Lauren Kenward. Thank you to my mother, María Orbelinda, and my sister, Linda María, for their love and support of my writing these last few years. Many thanks to the late, great Jeanne Córdova (aka Big Poppa) for her love and support; to Dr. Sandra Ruiz and the Minor Arts Laboratory at the University of Illinois Urbana-Champaign for supporting this work; and to the Center for Creative Photography for commissioning me to write poems for their *Chicana Photographers* exhibition. Three of those poems are featured in this collection. This labor was also generously supported by the Foundation for Contemporary Arts and United States Artists.

Thank you Rosa Alcalá, Jo Blair Cipriano, Nikki Darling, Mónica De La Torre, Dorothy Dávila, Angel Dominguez, Isaac Esposto, Marie Sarita Gaytan, Saúl Hernández Vargas, Susie Kantor, Leo Kim, Bojan Louis, Joseph Mains, Alyn Mare, Rubén Martínez, Eileen Cuthwulf Myles, mónica teresa ortiz, Ricardo L. Ortiz (RIP), Grace Rosario Perkins, Cristina Rivera Garza, Sandra Ruiz, Jeff Sirkin, Jared Stanley, Thea Quiray Tagle, Karen Tongson, Miranda Trimmier, Vanessa Angelica Villareal, and Javier Zamora, who, as my friends, served as shelter along the way through this period of interior restructuring.

A heartfelt shout-out to Alice Notley and Ricardo L. Ortiz, who passed away in the last year and have left me with their examples of how to lead every creative gesture with a deeper sense of care and generosity. I will continue to look to your lights for guidance.

And this work would be in no way possible without the love, care, and support by my most beloved reader, fellow traveler, and partner in life: Sandra K. Soto. I would drive the ends of the world for you. Te quiero chingos. Thank you for choosing me every day.

ABOUT THE AUTHOR

Raquel Gutiérrez is a poet, essayist, performer and the author of *Brown Neon: Essays* (Coffee House Press). Gutiérrez's work has been recently supported by the United States Artist Fellowship and the Foundation for Contemporary Arts Fellowship. Gutiérrez has lived on unceded lands of the Tohono O'odham and Pascua Yaqui people since 2016.